Seek and Find
SPACE

Illustrated by Emiliano Migliardo

BLOOMSBURY
Activity Books

Welcome to outer space!

Outer space is absolutely huge! People have been looking up at the stars and planets and wondering what might be up there for hundreds and hundreds of years. Even today we're still uncovering new things about it.

Life inside a space station

The International Space Station (ISS) is the biggest man-made object in space. Astronauts live and work inside of it. It has two bathrooms, a gym and lots of other rooms!

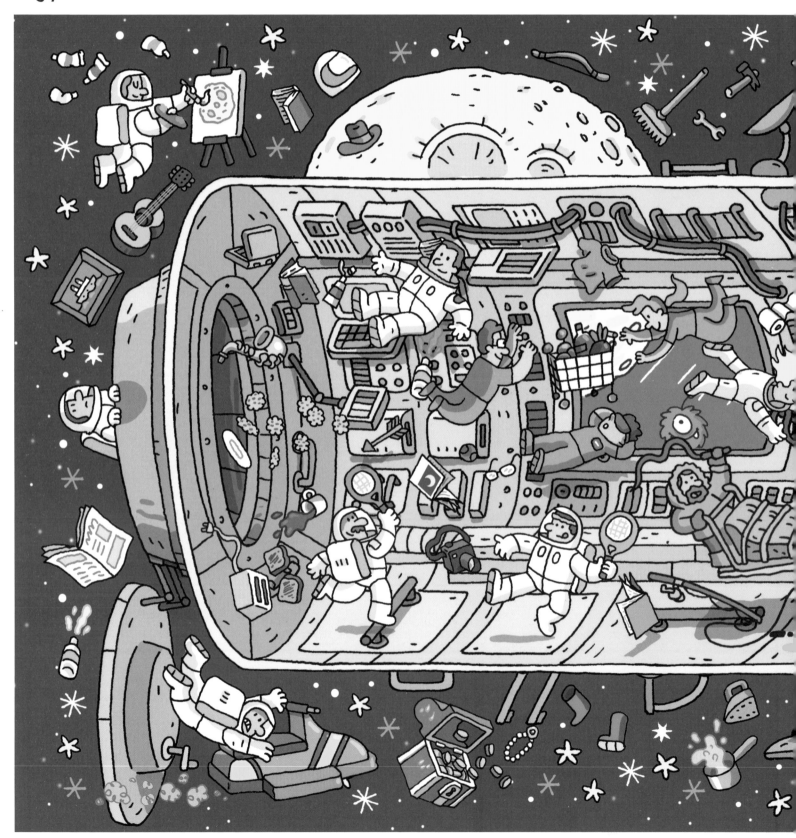

There's a wizard in the space station! Can you find him?

Can you find...

Awesome aliens!

People have wondered if there is life beyond planet Earth for hundreds of years. These friendly aliens are busy whizzing around – do you think astronauts will ever find them?

Can you spot the alien wearing red socks?

Can you find...

The solar system

The solar system is an exciting place and is full of planets, stars and much, much more. All of the planets in the Solar System orbit the Sun and our own planet Earth is one of them.

Can you spot the alien sunbathing?

Can you find...

Star gazing

There are countless things to see on a clear night. Here you can see the moon, comets, shooting stars, Northern Lights and much, much more!

A little mouse is trying to spot the North Star. Can you find him?

Can you find...

Outside the Space Station

Sometimes astronauts have to climb outside the station to do their work. There is less gravity in space than on Earth so they float about instead of walking!

One of the astronauts is having a barbeque. Can you find him?

Can you find...

A trip to the Moon!

People have been travelling to the Moon since 1969. The Moon travels around the Earth and takes around 27 days to do this!

Can you spot the astronaut on a broomstick?

Can you find...

Racing rockets!

Astronauts use lots of different ways to explore space. Some rockets have been used to send people all the way to the Moon.

One of the aliens has fallen upside down in his rocket! Can you spot him?

Can you find...

The Big Bang

Billions of years ago nothing at all existed. Then a giant explosion happened, called the Big Bang. This is how space and everything in it was created.

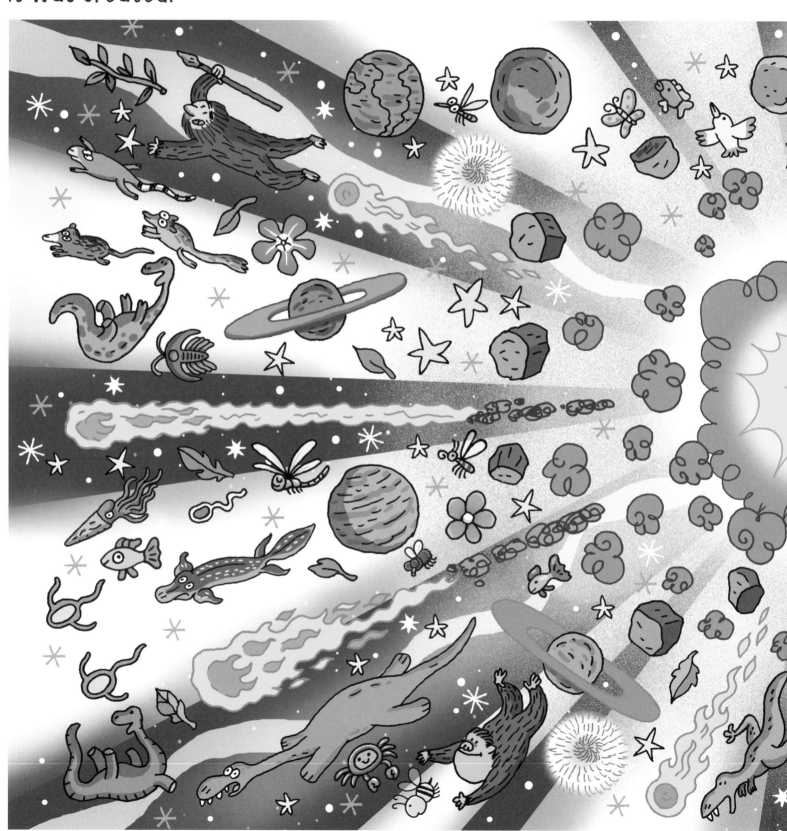

Can you spot the centipede?

Can you find...

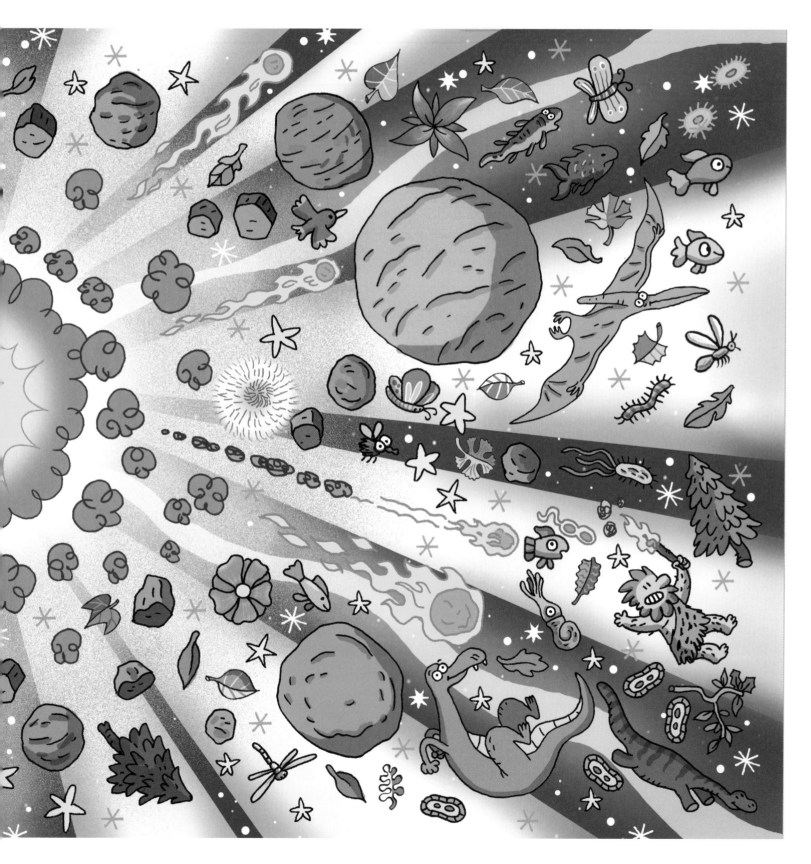

Party time!

The astronauts and aliens have got together to have a party!

One of the aliens is wearing glasses! Can you spot him?

Can you find...

The Milky Way

We live in a galaxy called the Milky Way. It is so big that it would take 100,000 years to get from one side to the other!

Can you spot the aliens on the rollercoaster?

Can you find...

SPACE FACTS

Gravity
Gravity is a force that means our feet stay on the ground! However, in space there is a lot less gravity so astronauts have to float from place to place instead of walking!

Food in space
Astronauts have to eat different food when they are in space. The food they eat can't make any crumbs that might float away.

Spacesuits
To survive in space, astronauts must wear special spacesuits. The suits stop astronauts from getting too hot or too cold and they also provide oxygen for them to breathe while they work in space. The suits can even hold water to drink!

Sleeping in space
Astronauts have to sleep in special sleeping bags. These are attached to the wall and ceilings so they don't float around while they are asleep and bump into things!

Exercise in space
Because astronauts float around instead of walking they don't use their legs very much. They have to exercise every day in order to keep their muscles and bones strong.

The Moon buggy
Astronauts sometimes use special machines to explore different planets even further. The Lunar Rover was driven by astronauts on the Moon and helped them collect samples of rocks, which gave scientists a much better understanding of the moon.

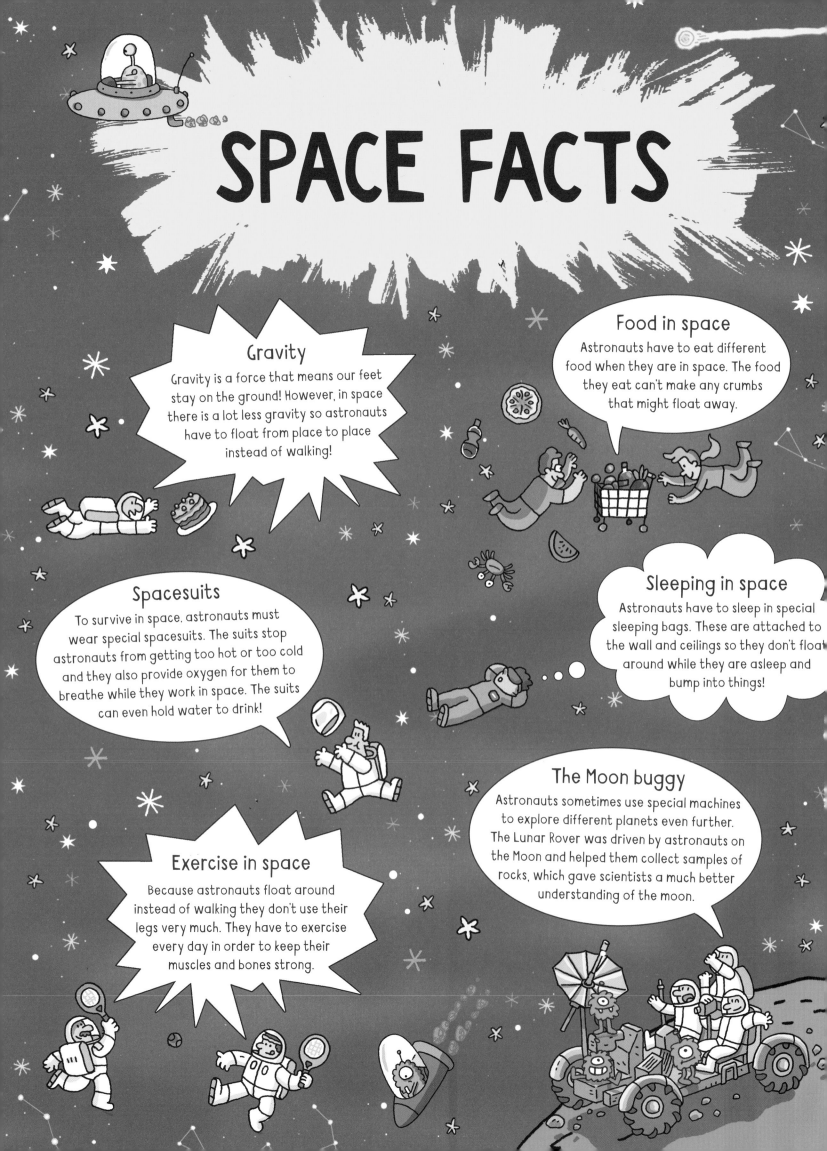